TATTING
Adventures
with
beads, shuttle & needle

TATTING
Adventures
with
beads, shuttle & needle

Judith Connors

LACIS PUBLICATIONS
Berkeley, CA USA

With loving thanks to Peter, my husband,
for his practical support, patience and encouragement

TATTING: ADVENTURES WITH BEADS, SHUTTLE AND NEEDLE

© 2000, Judith Connors

Cover and interior design: Anna Soo
Illustrations and photography: Judith Connors

Supplies
Full range of tatting shuttles in bone, shell, exotic woods and other fine
materials; needles for Needle Tatting, threads, accessories, books and videos:
    LACIS: 2982 Adeline Street, Berkeley, CA 94703
    Web: www.lacis.com

This edition published 2000 by
LACIS PUBLICATIONS
3163 Adeline Street
Berkeley, CA 94703 USA

ISBN: 1-891656-22-8

Printed in China

CONTENTS

PREFACE

Tatting is a very practical type of handmade lace. It can be put to many uses, both traditional and contemporary, and requires few implements for its manufacture. All one needs is one or two shuttles or needles, a ball of thread and clean hands. All these are very portable and can be taken out and used wherever and whenever the tatter desires.

During the twentieth century interest in shuttle tatting waxed and waned several times, following a period of popularity enjoyed at the close of the nineteenth century when it was used as a fashionable accessory as well as a trimming on clothing and soft furnishings. It declined in favour until the late 1920s, when interest was rekindled. In Australia, patterns created by Rachel Abraham, Muriel Arnold, Norma Benporath, D. Carroll, Hazel Frances, Ethel Thomson, Natalie Vandenbergh and others had tatters busy until well after World War II. It was similar in the United States, where designers like Angeline Hardwick Crichlow, Myrtle Hamilton and Anne Champe Orr produced patterns to challenge avid tatters.

With the more recent proliferation of handicrafts and greater interest in antiques, lace has come into vogue once more. New and colourful threads, and computer programs which facilitate pattern design, are challenging lace makers in the creation of modern and interesting pieces. The Internet enables a rapid and beneficial exchange of ideas. As a result of all these, tatting has developed and gained immensely. It is popular universally and has taken on an exciting contemporary style involving colour, threads and technique. This augurs well for its future in the twenty-first century.

The patterns in this book continue on from *Beads in Tatting* and combine traditional and contemporary styles and, of course, beads. Some techniques are common to a number of the projects. To save repetition of their descriptions within the specific chapters, they are set out in detail for your reference in a section on techniques beginning on page 16. You will also find there reference to the techniques of needle tatting and hook tatting. As needle tatters and hook tatters can use the same patterns as shuttle tatters, the word 'shuttle' may be replaced quite easily by either term in most patterns in this book.

I hope you find this collection challenging, and above all, enjoyable.

Judith Connors

Lace, lace, the grace of lace!
Rich are they who give it a place.
JMC

ON ADDING BEADS

It is possible to add beads everywhere tatting can be used—on traditional and contemporary designs, jewellery and accessories, party and bridal wear, furnishings, Christmas decorations, 3-dimensional work, collage—and with the variety of beads available today you can achieve beautiful effects.

The first thing to decide before adding beads to a piece of tatting is whether the beads are being used as focal points or as highlights. This will affect the sizes of the beads you choose and their placement. The weight of the thread will also influence the size of the beads you use, as it is not advisable to place large beads on light thread, nor tiny beads on a heavy thread.

Coloured beads will add interest as well, depending on the purpose of the piece of lace. Glass beads or crystals will sparkle in the light, pearls will add a lustre.

While many unusual forms may be found, beads come in a range of basic shapes:

| seed/rocaille | bugle | rice/barrel |
| round | teardrop | cut/facet |

Various shapes of beads

As some beads are not regular in shape, you may need to tat a trial piece of the pattern to determine how they will lie. Sometimes it may be necessary to change the beads or to alter the pattern to suit the shapes.

Sequins can be used in tatting also. They are added similarly to beads but, because of their shapes and sizes, will require planning before you include them. Notice the placement of the large round sequins in the photograph of the Angel Fish.

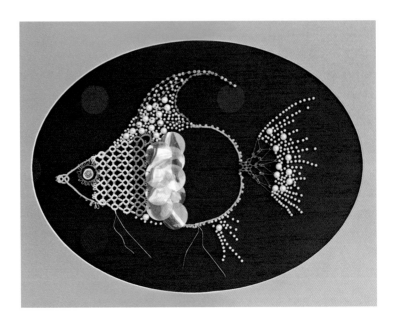

Angel Fish with large iridescent sequins

Although some modern beads are colourfast, there are others that may be affected by heat or laundering. For example, faux pearls and beads and sequins with an iridescent coating could react badly to washing. If there is any doubt, always test a sample few under conditions similar to those where they will be used.

As you are working, beads can be added in five ways:

- on the shuttle thread
- on the ball thread
- added to formed picots while joining
- on a separate thread
- added later to doubled shuttle or ball threads.

Each of these techniques is explained in the chapter on Techniques for the projects in which they are used.

If you wish to tat something for a special occasion, the following lists may be helpful in choosing beads of specific colours and compositions.

BIRTHSTONES

January	garnet	constancy, fidelity
February	amethyst	peace, sincerity
March	bloodstone	firmness, truth
April	diamond	purity, innocence
May	emerald	happiness
June	pearl	health, wealth
July	ruby	love, friendship
August	sardonyx	felicity
September	sapphire	wisdom
October	opal	inspiration, hope
November	topaz	creativity, awareness
December	turquoise	success, prosperity

ANNIVERSARY STONES AND METALS

china	2nd
crystal/glass	3rd
wood	5th
iron	6th
copper	7th
bronze	8th
tin/aluminium	10th
steel	11th
pearl	12th
ivory	14th
crystal	15th
china/platinum	20th
silver	25th
pearl/diamond	30th
coral/jade	35th
ruby	40th
sapphire	45th
emerald	55th
diamond	60th

USEFUL TIPS WITH BEADS

1. If you are using a lot of identical beads, add an extra one or two to the thread as you string them, just in case one breaks, or you have miscounted, or your tension is different from that of the pattern. The remaining beads may be removed when you have finished the lace.

2. It is a good practice to include the beads as you wind the thread on the shuttle. This spaces them out and eliminates constantly moving them backward on the spare thread as you work.

3. When you plan to include many beads in an article they may occupy a lot of space on the shuttle thread, thus it is advantageous to use a shuttle large enough to accommodate both thread and beads. Large plastic shuttles are available from some craft suppliers, but a suitable one can be cut out of firm scrap plastic (e.g. milk or detergent bottles) using the pattern below, enlarged or reduced as required. Wind the thread around the inside prong and through the tip from front to back.

Pattern for a large shuttle

4. It is always wise to block or size your finished piece of lace as a final touch. See Presentation of Work on page 28. Handling the piece and the addition of beads can distort its shape slightly, so pin it out carefully to size and shape. Use pins that will neither rust nor leave marks and insert them perpendicular to the surface used. Spray a light mist of water over the piece and leave it to dry thoroughly before removing

the pins. To hasten the drying of smaller pieces of tatting a hair dryer could be used, but only on minimum setting at some distance above the lace.

5. When you use a stiffening medium on lace with beads, always blot the beads very well to remove any residual liquid that would dull their shine or lustre.

6. Allow articles that have been stiffened to dry in a dust-free environment.

7. Sometimes you may be unable to insert a needle through the holes in small beads. Here are two solutions to the problem:
   - Add a little nail varnish to the end of the cotton and, when this is dry thread, the beads as if using a needle.
   - If the beads are already strung, make the first half of an overhand knot at the end of their thread, catching the shuttle/ball thread through the knot before drawing it closed. Then slide the beads from their string, over the knot, onto the shuttle/ball thread.

8. To prevent round beads rolling about on smooth surfaces, place them on a square of felt.

9. In patterns where rice beads are required, 2 or 3 smaller round beads may be substituted for each rice bead.

SYMBOLS AND ABBREVIATIONS

SYMBOLS FOR VISUAL PATTERNS

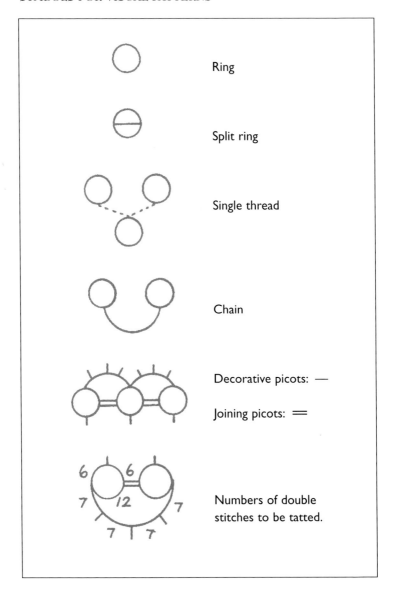

Ring

Split ring

Single thread

Chain

Decorative picots: —

Joining picots: =

Numbers of double stitches to be tatted.

ABBREVIATIONS

ds	= double stitch
ch	= chain
p	= picot
r	= ring
RW	= reverse work*
T	= turn*
cl	= close
j	= join
lj	= lock join
beg	= beginning
sh	= shuttle
prev	= previous
sp	= small picot
sm	= small
lp	= large picot
mp	= measured picot
sep	= separated
sr	= split ring
CTM	= continuous thread method, i.e. do not cut the thread after winding the shuttle; this is sometimes shown as O—O when using two shuttles.
WWT	= wrong way tatting. This is made the usual way but without transferring the knot. The stitches thus formed will not slide on the thread of the shuttle making them. It is sometimes called 'reverse stitch'.

Notes
*RW denotes reversing the lace with a top-to-bottom movement, whereas T indicates a right-to-left movement as if turning the page of a book.

A *spacer* is a piece of card or plastic of a specific width to measure picots or spaces. If you cut your own, be sure to write its width on it for future reference.

TECHNIQUES

These techniques are common to many of the projects in this book. To save repetition of their descriptions within the specific patterns, they are set out here once in detail for your reference. You may find them useful when designing your own articles as well.

BASIC METHODS WITH BEADS

Beads may be placed where picots appear in any pattern. You can add single or multiple beads in any one spot. Depending on whether the picots are on rings or chains, the beads must be threaded on the shuttle or the ball thread prior to starting the lace. The number of beads required will be ascertained by a study of the pattern. Should you want to mix colours, work out the pattern and thread the beads in the inverse order to the way you will work them into your lace, that is, thread the last bead on first and the first bead on last.

Method 1: On rings

As rings are formed differently when tatting on a needle, this method applies principally to shuttle tatting. Prior to starting any pattern, string all the beads you will need on the rings onto the shuttle thread. When tatting each ring, include the required number of beads inside the thread as you wrap it around your hand *before* the first double stitch. Then slide them up as you reach the picots. All stitches should fit snugly beside the beads.

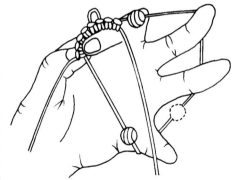

Beads on the ring thread

Method 2: On chains

Before you start any pattern, string all beads needed on chains onto the ball thread. When tatting a chain, just slide the required number of beads along the ball thread as you reach the position selected. This method will be the most common one used when tatting on a needle as, generally, the double stitches of both rings and chains are formed using the ball thread.

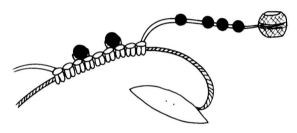

Beads on the ball thread

Method 3: On formed picots

You may add loose beads as you join a ring or a chain to a formed picot. In this case, the picot should be long enough to accommodate the bead/s and the join. You will also need a crochet hook fine enough to go through the holes in the beads.

As you reach each join, place a bead on the crochet hook, catch it over the formed picot and slide the bead/s onto it. With the hook still in the picot, draw the passive thread of the ring or chain up through the end of the picot to form a small loop. Then pass the shuttle or needle through the loop to make a normal join.

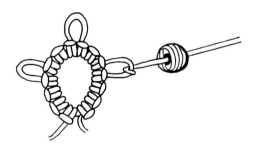

Bead on the crochet hook

17

Method 4: Inside a ring

This is a variation on Method 3. The idea is, while tatting a ring, to create a picot long enough to accommodate a bead and span the centre of the ring when it is closed. As this long picot will have to be joined diagonally opposite itself before all the double stitches have been completed, form it early in the ring pattern.

Begin tatting any ring as illustrated, adding an extra long picot to the given pattern. Continue the double stitches until you are diagonally opposite the long picot. Then fold this picot behind the ring and thread on the required bead with the aid of a crochet hook. With the hook still in the picot, place it over the passive thread and draw this through the end of the picot to form a loop. Remove the crochet hook and pass the shuttle through the loop. Ease this down gently beside the other double stitches so that the shuttle thread will still run through them all. Make the second half of a double stitch. Finish the ring according to the pattern and close. The bead should lie in the centre of the ring.

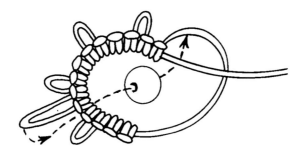

Unfinished ring, long picot and bead

Method 5: On a separate thread

By using this method you can add a string of beads between two adjoining rows of rings or chains. The beads will zigzag between the rows. Bugle beads, rice beads or pairs of smaller beads will create an eye-catching effect, whether you tat with a needle or a shuttle. Thread all the beads in readiness and loosely anchor them with an overhand knot at each end. Begin tatting the first

18

of the two adjoining rows and attach one end of the string of beads to the top of the first ring/chain. Continue with your pattern until you arrive at the next point of attachment. Leave a pair of beads and then make a join. Continue in this manner till you have finished the row. Tat the second row, joining the rings/chains between each pair of beads on the separate thread. As you work along you can adjust the tension of this thread so that everything is balanced by the end of the second row.

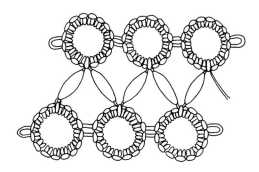

Beads zigzagging between rows

SPLIT RING

Developed around 1923 by Anne Champe Orr, the split ring did not become really popular until the 1980s. Anne Orr called it 'reverse stitch', and directions for making it were given in the re-publications of her patterns: *Anne Orr's Classic Tatting Patterns* (1985) and *Tatting with Anne Orr* (1989). Perhaps you have copies. Her original books were published circa 1935 and 1940. There were, however, no guidelines for the split ring's application, neither was there any reference to it in her patterns. Over time reverse stitch has also been called 'wrong way tatting'.

Mary Sue Kuhn renamed the technique 'split ring' and promoted it in her book, *The Joy of Split Ring Tatting* (1984). The patterns she designed were composed mostly of lines of rings using two shuttles with threads of differing colours.

Today tatters universally enjoy the benefits of the split ring. It has developed from the decorative uses mentioned above to wider applications. Now tatters can climb out of central rings, make a braid of rings end-to-end, proceed from one motif to another, and move to a following row of work, all without ending off and beginning again. In the diagrams below, the heavier lines indicate the wrong way tatting of shuttle 2.

Various ring formations

Experienced tatters will realise how split rings may be used in their old favourite patterns to avoid ends and to save time and thread. This proves quite beneficial.

The split ring technique requires two shuttles which usually contain threads of equal thicknesses, for example, 40 and 40, 60 and 60. With shuttle 1 tat the first part of the ring normally, and then with shuttle 2 form reverse stitches or wrong way tatting for the other portion. These reverse stitches are made the usual way, but without the transfer of the knot, thus enabling the thread of shuttle 1 to slide through all double stitches of the ring.

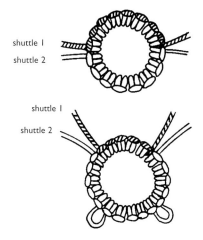

shuttle 1
shuttle 2

shuttle 1
shuttle 2

Split rings showing two sets of stitches

There is no need to take the ring off your hand for part 2. After tatting with shuttle 1, just turn your hand to expose the thread between the thumb and the little finger. Adjust the tension if necessary so this thread remains taut. Take up shuttle 2 and tat reverse stitches along this thread. To preserve the right-side effect of the ring, reverse the order of the halves of the double stitches, that is, start with the second half-stitch. Picots can be made as usual where required.

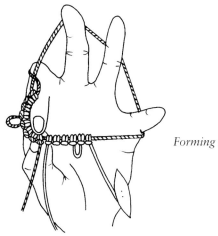

Forming wrong way tatting

When the ring is complete, remove it from around your hand and close it normally with shuttle 1. Continue with the pattern being worked.

TATTED SQUARES

Tatted squares are ornamental sections that consist of a number of short rows of chain worked backwards and forwards closely upon one another. Each row is built upon the previous one with the double stitches standing in the same direction. The number of double stitches per row generally corresponds to the number of rows. For example, for a square of 5 rows there should be 5 double stitches per chain row. Tatted squares are sometimes wrongly referred to as 'tallies', as they differ completely in execution from the leaf-shaped tallies of Cluny tatting.

Tatted squares may follow on from a ring, a split ring (see Fleur, page 74), a chain (see Marguerite, page 41) or another tatted square. In any instance there should be a small picot or space just before the first chain row. It is sometimes handy to insert a safety pin to form a starter picot or space before commencing the square. Your tension will have to be slightly looser than normal as the chains formed need to be straight, not curved. To preserve the tension in a preceding chain, tat a lock stitch (a first half-stitch in WWT) before starting the first row of the square.

Before adding a tatted square to your patterns, it is wise to work out the direction from which you require the threads to come *after* the square is finished. For right-handed tatters odd-numbered chain rows bring the threads to the right, even-numbered rows bring them to the left, as shown in the two directional diagrams.

Directions of 5- and 6-rowed squares

For this example 5 chains of 5 double stitches will be used.

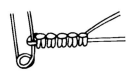

You will need two shuttles, referred to as Sh.1 and Sh.2. The thread may be continuous or issue from one of the positions in your lace mentioned above. Make a small picot or pass the threads around a safety pin and tat 5ds with Sh.1. Turn work (right to left). Change shuttles.

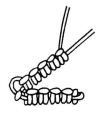

With Sh.2 tat one half-stitch, preferably the second half, to act as an elbow joint, 1 small picot and 5ds for the second chain. Then remove the safety pin.

With a crochet hook catch the chain thread* of Sh.1 from the back, and draw it through the starter picot to form a loop. Pass Sh.2 through the loop and ease the threads down so the work lies flat. Turn work and change shuttles.

Using Sh.1, tat 1 half-stitch (elbow), 1 small picot, 5ds. Then join as before to the picot of chain 2. Continue making the square until the end of chain 5 where, this time, you can use a normal shuttle/lock join. If your tension is sufficiently loose, your chains should be straight and lie parallel, forming a solid square.

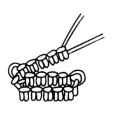

Tatted square sequence

---

*Some tatters use a shuttle or lock join here, but this results in open loops forming at the sides of the square.

There are two techniques referred to as needle tatting. While both present finished work similar to that made with a shuttle, in order to distinguish the one from the other references to them will be to tatting *with* a needle and to tatting *on* a needle.

1 With a needle

During the nineteenth century Mlle Eléonore Riego referred to tatting with a needle in her early published patterns, circa 1850. Often she used a threaded needle to make joins between rings and rows in pieces she had designed. This 'Needle Period' was regarded as transitional, as the developments of joining rings and of making chains as they were being tatted superseded it. Refer to *Beeton's Book of Needlework* by Isabella Beeton (1870; facsimile edition 1986), *Tatting: Technique and History* by Elgiva Nicholls (1962) and *The Complete Book of Tatting* by Rebecca Jones (1985).

Today, however, some tatters find using a needle (sewing, tapestry, wool, bodkin) preferable to a shuttle, even though they follow the same technique of wrapping the ring and chain threads around the opposite hand. Fewer fingers need to be employed in the wrap, which may benefit people with arthritis, and children with small hands. When making the first modern half-stitch, the hand using the needle does not have to raise the thread as high as would be required to allow the passage of a shuttle. Others use a needle simply because they cannot master a shuttle.

Once the needle has formed each loop, the 'transfer' and the positioning of half-stitches proceed as in shuttle tatting.

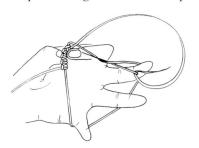
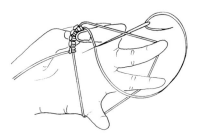

Forming the first half-stitch   *Forming the second half-stitch*

Needles can be more convenient where short lengths of thread exist, or are needed. They are handy when making the second half of a split chain instead of using the Dora Young method with a shuttle. Very fine threads can be used with a needle where the same threads may be damaged when passing between the tips of a shuttle. Refer to *New Dimensions in Tatting* by To de Haan-van Beek (English translation 1994).

Some teachers of tatting show beginners this method with a needle first, and once the transfer of the loop is mastered, introduce the shuttle. Of course, sometimes experienced tatters use needle tatting, and even finger tatting, in conjunction with a shuttle. It all depends on what they plan to achieve.

2 On a needle

The second technique was developed more recently, and is used in Scandinavian countries, the USA, Australia and New Zealand. It requires pairs of half-hitches, or cow hitches, to be placed along a needle of regular gauge. Refer to Rebecca Jones' *Complete Book of Tatting* (1985) and to *Learn Needle Tatting Step-by-Step* by Barbara Foster (1998). While a suitable darning needle or a bodkin could be used, a set of needles is generally required, as in crochet and knitting. These range in size from #0 to #9 (thickest to finest), and threads/yarns are matched accordingly. In the late 1970s Selma and Ed Morin of Oregon, USA, developed a similar technique which they called Jiffy Tatting. They also produced a set of Jiffy Needles. Refer to their book, *The Complete Book of Jiffy Needle Tatting*, KC Publishing Inc. (1992).

While tatting on a needle is not intended to replace shuttle tatting, it has proven very popular because of its ease of formation. This is good for children and those who lack manual dexterity. Another advantage is the additional use of fluffy, soft threads. Two needles may be employed similarly to two shuttles. It does, however, differ from shuttle tatting in technique. A single or a doubled thread may carry the stitches, with the doubled thread giving the finished work a padded appearance.

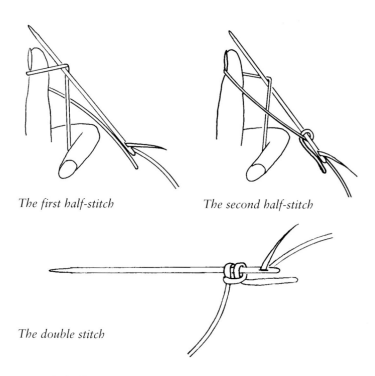

The first half-stitch　　　　　*The second half-stitch*

The double stitch

Each half-stitch is generally made by looping the ball thread around the index finger or thumb, and then placing the loop so formed over the free end of the needle. This technique is similar to one known method of casting on stitches for knitting. Picots, as in shuttle tatting, are measured spaces between two double stitches. A picot join is made directly onto the needle by simply lifting a loop of thread through the adjacent picot. An advantage of tatting on a needle is the ease with which mistakes can be undone. Stitches are just slipped off the needle and remade.

Almost every technique in shuttle tatting can be replicated by tatting on a needle, though the latter is slightly looser in appearance. Patterns for shuttle tatting, especially the contemporary visual ones, can be followed easily. In practice, however, most tatting on a needle is actually a series of chains, with some being drawn close together to form mock rings. This practice is not unknown in shuttle tatting, in fact whole patterns can be done with it, but mock rings are quite different from actual rings. Patterns featuring rings solely are the only ones where actual rings are formed with a needle. A single carrying thread would be advisable in this case, to avoid doubled thread between the rings. The tatter starts at the end of the thread and works towards the needle. As no ball is required this thread would need renewing more frequently.

HOOK TATTING

This is a form of tatting which developed in Japan. It uses a round shaft of regular gauge with a hook at each end. It resembles a double-ended crochet hook, but the hooks have been flattened to reduce any bulk while working. As with a tatting needle, the gauge of each tatting hook depends on the thickness of yarn being used.

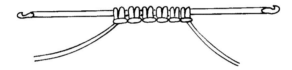

Double stitches on a tatting hook

The technique for making double stitches is exactly the same as that for tatting on a needle (see Needle Tatting, above.) However, because there is a hook at either end, the tatting hook may pass both ways through the double stitches, drawing loops of yarn after it. Tatters who use this technique can still follow patterns written for shuttle and needle tatting.

There is yet another form of tatting which utilises an ordinary crochet hook. It developed in the late nineteenth century but is rarely used today. Known as *tatting crochet*, it is a hybrid technique using both hook tatting and crochet.

PRESENTATION OF WORK

While most tatters make their lace for pleasure to use personally or as gifts, some may wish to enter their pieces in shows and exhibitions. Naturally, all would like their lace to look its best. The following are suggestions to present your lace well, no matter what you intend to do with it.

- Always have clean hands to make your lace, and an environment free of fluff and dust. When you are not working at it, wrap your lace in a clean cloth. Remember, pieces for competition must not be washed.

- Always work in good light, especially with very fine thread. Depending on the colour of your thread, have a plain contrasting background on your lap so the stitches and joins will be easy to see. This relieves the eyes as well.

- As a general rule, choose threads that are mercerised and have a tight twist in their ply. These produce crisp tatting. While threads with a looser ply may be good for cut and frayed picots, they tend to separate around the curves of picots in normal work. However, your choice of threads will ultimately depend on the effect you wish to create with your piece.

- Have a pair of sharp embroidery scissors so you can cut threads off cleanly and neatly. Unless it is your intended effect, avoid frayed, fluffy ends. Try to keep these scissors exclusively for cutting threads so their blades remain keen.

- Develop a firm even tension throughout your work.

- Rings, unless stated in the pattern, must be closed completely. There should be no spaces between the rings of 3- and 4-leaved clovers.

- Keep the size of your decorative picots regular. To avoid floppy work make your joining picots reasonably small.

- No matter which method you choose, end off well and unobtrusively.

- If you tat a pattern which consists of a number of discrete motifs, be sure that you have them all facing to the same side of the finished work.

- Once your piece is finished, block or size it for a crisp appearance. Blocking really improves its presentation. (See Useful tips, 4, on page 12). If your piece is large, press or block it at intervals while tatting to maintain the correct shape. Cover the lace with a cloth before pressing it on the wrong side. Avoid pressing the right side as this will flatten the work.

- It is a useful practice to leave ends of 2 cm (1 inch) after finishing a row. This will ensure that any movement while working will not unravel or fray any threads you have cut. As dampening the lace while blocking causes a slight shrinkage, this will tighten around the ends that have been left. When the whole piece is finished the ends can be cut off cleanly before presentation.

- The traditional right side of a piece of tatting is the ring side and the chain side is the wrong side. Be aware, however, that contemporary tatting can combine these on the front of the work by reversing the order of the half-stitches when tatting the chain. To maintain the regular appearance of the lark's head knots, some picot joins may have to be made downwards. All this is a personal choice, but it can change the appearance of your work slightly. Try it sometime when you wish a piece to be viewed from one side only.

  If you want to achieve a front-side-only effect on a small section, try using wrong way or reverse stitch tatting along the chain with a second shuttle, just as you would with a split ring. There is no need to reverse your work if you use this technique.

THE PATTERNS

ACACIA
A DELIGHTFUL BEADED BAG

Materials
1 shuttle, or #5–#7 needle
No. 20–40 thread
seed pearls, 10 per motif
crochet hook
20 cm (8 inches) fabric
fusible interfacing
snap fastener
1.25 m (48 inches) matching cord or chain (optional)

Acacia

Here is an accessory which may be worn as a clutch or shoulder bag. The motif repeated throughout the lace is quite easy, so tatters of any level can attempt it. The pattern may be lengthened or widened, so extra motifs can be added as required. On the bag illustrated there are 16 motifs, requiring 160 seed pearls/beads. The trim around the bottom is optional and lends itself to your creativity.

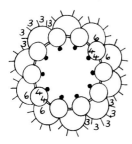

The basic motifs have 10 rings and chains each and are assembled by the picots indicated in the diagram below. Before starting each motif place 10 seed pearls/beads onto the ball thread. Then wind the beads with 3 m (3¼ yds) from the ball onto the shuttle CTM. Space the beads out as you go. Refer to Method 1 (page 16) for adding beads to tatted rings. All rings

The basic motif

have 6ds, p/join, 4ds, bead, 4ds, p, 6ds. Chains have 3ds, (p, 3ds) 4 times. *Note*: When making the lace regard the chain side as the right side so that the finished picots will lie flat against the fabric; or you could tat the motifs with a definite front and back.

To make the bag, cut 3 ovals of fabric and 3 ovals of fusible interfacing. Two of the fabric ovals will be machine-sewn together to form the outer and inner sides of the bag, while the third will be folded in half and sewn on to form the pocket.

The scale of the pattern diagram is 1 square = 2.5 cm (1 inch). A seam allowance of 1 cm (³/₈ inch) is included in the pattern.

Follow the product instructions and iron the interfacing onto the wrong side of each piece of fabric.

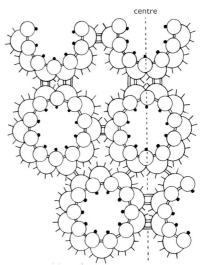

How to assemble the motifs

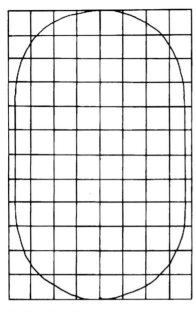

Scale-reduced pattern

With the right sides facing, sew 2 ovals together, leaving a space at one end through which to turn them to the right side. Clip around the curve or trim with pinking shears, as these notch the edge nicely. Turn right-side out carefully and press the seams flat. Fold the third oval in half, right-side inwards. Sew around this similarly and turn to the right side. Attach the pocket to the inner side of the bag by oversewing invisibly along the seams. Then position the lace on the outside, tack it on lightly, and carefully hand sew the lace to the fabric. Add the snap fastener to keep the flap closed.

The trim around the bottom of the bag is a continuous tatted chain with 3-bead drops. Chain 4ds, long p, 3ds, add the set of 3 beads to the long picot and then reattach it to the chain, 4ds. This is a variation of Method 3 on page 17. The formed picots are 1 cm (³/₈ inch) in length. The single beads on some chains were added to the ball thread before tatting the trim. Refer to Method 2 on page 17.

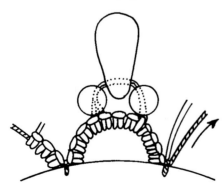

You can trim the bag with whatever strikes your fancy, narrow fringing perhaps. Lastly, if you want it, attach the shoulder cord. Now make a reservation for an evening out!

Three beads on a formed picot

PASQUALE
A DECORATIVE EGG

Materials
1 shuttle
No. 20 cotton of chosen colour
18 small beads
1 m (1 yd) contrasting thread
crochet hook
empty egg, blown or plastic

Mounted egg

Here is an attractive gift for a friend at Easter, or just as a decorative piece in a suitable rest. There are two tatted halves

33

which are laced together with a contrasting or metallic thread. As the lace is meant to be viewed from one side only, the rings and the chains should be tatted on the right side. If you wish, you could dye or paint the egg before attaching the lace.

The central ring and the two rows around it are made on a continuous shuttle thread. So wind 4 m (4½ yds) of thread onto the shuttle. *Note*: All picots, except for the decorative ones on the outside chain, are to be quite small, much smaller than in the flattened visual pattern. Refer to Method 2 on page 17 for adding beads on a ball thread.

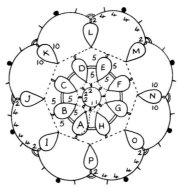

Visual pattern

Leaving a loose end of 12 cm (5 inches), form a ring as illustrated: 1ds, (p, 2ds) 7 times, p, 1ds. The loose end will be used later to thread a bead and attach it across the centre of the ring before ending off.

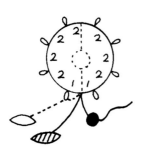

The central ring

With the crochet hook, draw the shuttle thread up through the first picot and make a shuttle/lock join. Work the first round of rings (A–H), joining the shuttle thread closely to the next inner picot after closing each ring. Each ring has 5ds, p/join, 5ds, p, 5ds, p, 5ds. When round 1 is complete, join the thread to the first picot once more.

Then, at the back, slip the thread up to the top of ring A, making a shuttle/lock join in the picot between A and H and another in the picot at the top of A. You are now ready to tat the second round of rings (I–P), 10ds, p, 10ds. As you do, leave sufficient length on the thread so that each ring of this round will fit almost halfway across the space between each pair of rings in round 1. Your work should become slightly cup-shaped. When round 2 is complete, end off.

Before working the outside chain CTM, thread 8 beads onto the ball thread and then wind 75 cm (30 inches) onto the shuttle, keeping the beads on the ball side. *Do not cut the thread.* With a shuttle/lock join attach the thread to the picot at the top of ring I and tat the chain as illustrated, 2ds, sm p/join, 4ds, p, 4ds, bead, 4ds, p, 4ds, sm p, 2ds. Keep the tension firm and you will find that the lace will become more cup-shaped. When round 3 is complete, end off.

Return to the centre of the piece. Take the loose end to the back of the work and thread on 1 bead. Draw the thread across the centre, positioning the bead, and sew the end to the opposite side.

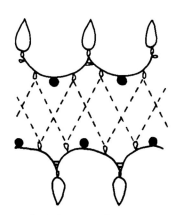

Lacing the halves together

Make a second piece to match.

Once the lace is worked you are ready to arrange the two pieces on either end of your egg. As you do make sure the beads on each piece are diagonally opposite one another. A little glue at the extremities of the egg should help to hold the lace in place. Using the contrasting thread, lace across the space around the middle, catching this thread through the picots of the chains. You will have to go around twice to form the diamond effect. Tie the ends and finish off. Your egg may be hung or mounted in a decorative rest.

ENYA
A PLAITED BRAID

Materials
6 shuttles or 3 needles
threads in 3 colours equivalent to No. 20 cotton
crochet hook

Belt with plaited braid

Do not take fright at the number of shuttles or needles required for this braid, as the basic pattern is really easy. You can tat a piece as long as you wish. All that you will need to master is the order for working the plaited strands before joining the rings along each side. The braid on this belt was worked with 3 skeins of rayon equivalent to No. 20 cotton. It is 2.5 cm (1 inch) wide

36

and 57 cm (22½ inches) long. No matter which threads you choose, they must all be the same thickness.

For each strand or colour you will need 1 average-sized shuttle and 1 large shuttle. Refer to page 12 for the pattern for a large shuttle you can make yourself and cut 3 of them. When you prepare the shuttles, wind twice as much thread on the larger shuttle as you put on the smaller one. For example, should you choose a skein of rayon which contains 18 metres, wind 12 metres on the larger shuttle and then, CTM, the remaining 6 metres onto the smaller shuttle. If you tat on a needle you will only have to work out the length of carrying thread required for each needle. The remainder will stay on the ball or skein.

Each strand follows a basic pattern. The small shuttle is Sh.1 and the large shuttle, Sh.2. With Sh.1 make a ring of 4ds, p (or join to adjacent ring), 8ds, p, 4ds. RW. Chain 12ds. With Sh.2 tat a ring of 4ds, p (or join to adjacent ring), 8ds, p, 4ds. Change to Sh.1 and chain 12ds. RW and continue the pattern with another strand. For coarser threads, the rings can be 3—6—3. Hasten slowly in order to plait the strands before joining the rings. The finished braid will be worth the care.

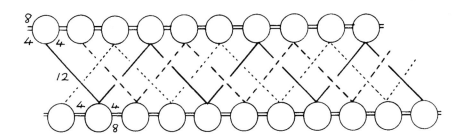

The plaited strands

When the shuttles for two of the strands are not in use, keep them on either side of you. Sit on them if you want, but this is not advisable for needle tatters!

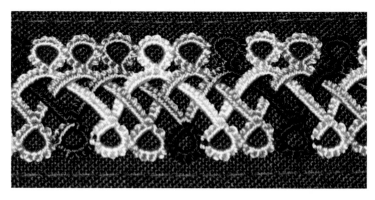

Enya close-up

If you plan to mount this braid onto a surface, as on the belt in the photograph, you may want to make a definite right and wrong side to your work. As the chains and their rings compose the major part of this piece, regard the chain side (Sh.2) as the right side and adjust the other row of rings (Sh.1) accordingly. To maintain the regular appearance of the double stitches or lark's head knots, some rings may be joined with downward loops.

NOËL
A FESTIVE STAR

Materials
1 shuttle or #5–#7 needle
No. 20 thread
10 seed beads (optional)
metal bangle 7 cm (2½ inches) in diameter
fine crochet hook

Noël

This piece, when finished, measures 8.5 cm (3⅜ inches) in diameter. It may be tatted totally white, or with a mixture of seasonal colours.

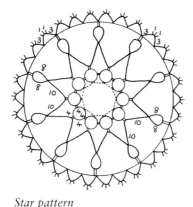

Star pattern

Row 1: Wind approximately 2 m (2¼ yds) of thread onto the shuttle and tat 10 rings. Leave a 2 mm (¹⁄₁₂ inch) length of thread before starting each new ring, and keep the joining picots between rings fairly small. Each ring has 4ds, p/join, 4ds, p, 4ds, p, 4ds. Tie and end off. If you are tatting on a needle, use only a needle thread and start at the free end.

Row 2: CTM: Wind a generous 2.5 m (2¾ yds) of thread onto the shuttle. *Do not cut the thread from the ball.* There are 10 rings of 8ds, p, 8ds. When tatting the chains, try to keep a medium tension so that they are almost straight. If your bangle is slightly different in size from the measurement given, you may need to reduce or increase the number of ds on the chains. Tat 10ds, join to the picot of a ring in Row 1, 10ds. If you wish, add a seed bead to the picot when making this join. Refer to Method 3 on page 17. Continue the pattern. Tie and end off. Keep the spare thread on your shuttle, but check that its length is at least 3 times the circumference of the bangle. Block the star so it will fit inside the bangle, and so the points are at regular distances apart.

Row 3: Using the crochet hook, attach the ball thread to the bangle, and immediately join in one of the outer rings of the star. Crochet around the metal bangle, joining in the remaining outer rings at appropriate intervals. Do not end off nor cut the thread once you have completely covered the bangle.

Row 4: Discard the crochet hook for the moment. Join in the thread on the shuttle and then tat the chains around the outside of the crochet, attaching them with shuttle joins at appropriate intervals (3 per space between rings). End off.

Attach a hanger and a tassel, and place the decoration on your tree, or in a position where the breeze will make it rotate.

MARGUERITE
A BOUQUET OF DAISIES

Materials
2 shuttles
thread of your choice*
crochet hook

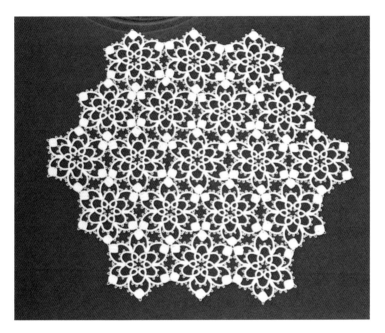

Marguerite doily

The inclusion of solid tatted squares adds a different texture to this lace doily. Refer to Tatted Squares on page 22.

*While you may choose any thickness of thread, the piece illustrated was worked in No. 20 cotton and is 28 cm (11 inches) wide. Each hexagonal motif in this design can be tatted CTM, if you so wish. Using No. 20 thread, you will require 2.75 m (3 yds) on Sh.1 and 3.75 m (4 yds) on Sh.2. Otherwise, just fill both shuttles and make a join as you start each new motif.

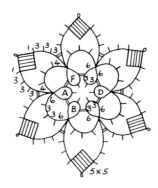

Motif with squares

Round 1: This round is quite simple. All rings have 6ds, p/join, 3ds, p, 3ds, p, 6ds. Chains have 6ds, p, 3ds, p, 3ds, p, 6ds. Once you have completed the 6th chain, use the crochet hook in drawing up a loop of the shuttle thread between the base of ring A and the first chain. Make a shuttle/lock join and position it well. Lock joins will be made at all other similar points of the motif when working Round 2.

Round 2: Chain 4ds, p, 3ds, p, 3ds, p, 3ds, p, 1ds. Tension this chain well and then tat a first half-stitch in WWT. This effectively locks in the tension before you start the tatted square. Tat one square of 5 rows of 5ds. The picot at the upper tip of the square is formed by enlarging the tiny picot after the last elbow joint. (*Note:* As some of these enlarged picots will become joining points for 3 motifs, avoid making them too large or the doily will become floppy.) Then complete the chain, 1ds, p, 3ds, p, 3ds, p, 3ds, p, 4ds. Make a lock join at the base of the next ring. Continue the pattern until you have 6 such chains containing tatted squares. End off the motif.

There are 19 motifs in this hexagonal doily. Seven motifs will form a smaller doily. With a little planning you can build up other shapes, even a lacy vest for yourself.

REGINA
A BRIDAL CORONET

Materials
2 shuttles or #5–#7 needle
No. 20 white thread
crochet hook
108 seed pearls
metal ring 10 cm (4 inches) in diameter
white florist's tape or ribbon
stiffening medium

Regina

Here is something totally different to top off a bridal veil. This coronet adds a regal touch and may be made in any size. It is composed of four rows of tatting. After you have covered the metal ring firmly with white florist's tape or ribbon, the outer circumference will equal the length of lace needed. The coronet illustrated was tatted in No. 20 cotton thread as this absorbs the stiffening medium quite well.

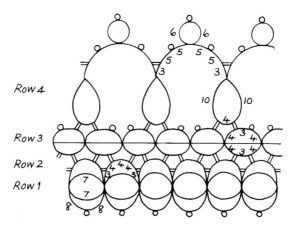

Bridal coronet

Row 1: This is the row that sits against the covered metal ring. It is worked with one shuttle and a ball thread. String at least 36 seed pearls onto the ball thread before starting. Refer to Method 2 on page 17 for beads on chains. As you tat the rings ensure the picots are quite small so that the lace is firm. Individual tensions differ, but an even number of small tatted rings will be required for the pattern.

Each ring has 7ds, sm p, 7ds. RW. Chain 8ds, seed pearl, 8ds, shuttle join to the sm p of the preceding ring. RW. When you have tatted the length you need, create a circle by making a shuttle/lock join to first ring. Do not end off. Reverse your work so the pearls are on the bottom. Any spare pearls may be left on the ball thread until the end of Row 2.

Row 2: This row is entirely chain with lock joins into the picots of Row 1. Chain 3ds, sm p/join, 4ds, p, 4ds, p, 4ds, sm p, 3ds. When this row is complete, end off. Remove the remaining seed pearls of Row 1.

Row 3: Two shuttles will be needed here for the split rings. Refer to Split Ring on page 19. Sh.1 will join onto Row 2 and Sh.2 will position the pearls. On Sh.2 string as many seed pearls as you used for Row 1. Arrange the lace upside down so that the pearls of Row 1 are uppermost and the picots of Row 2 are just above where you will be tatting with Sh.1. Tat this row in pairs of rings so that the positions of the pearls and the picots reverse order. *Shuttle 1*: 4ds, join to second p of one chain, 3ds, join to first p of next chain, 4ds. *Shuttle 2* in WWT: 4ds, slide a pearl into place just as you would for a chain, 3ds, p, 4ds. On the following ring change the positions of the pearl and the picot. Continue making split rings around the row. End off by joining to the first ring.

Row 4: Two shuttles will be needed here, too. Sh.2 will become the ball thread for the chains, and will also form the small rings on top of the chains, so all seed pearls will go on Sh.2. You will require as many as you used in Row 1 *plus* half as many again. Refer to Methods 2 and 1 on pages 16 and 17 for beads on chains and on rings. Using Sh.1, join the large rings to the free picots of each pair of split rings of Row 3. This forms a clover effect.

Keep the lace upside down and begin where there is a pair of picots. *Shuttle 1*: Tat a ring of 10ds, join to the first picot, 4ds, join to the second picot, 10ds. RW. Chain 3ds, sm p/join, 5ds, slide up a pearl, 5ds. Change shuttles. *Shuttle 2*: Slide up a pearl and include it as you wrap the thread around your hand. Refer to Method 1. Tat a ring of 6ds, pearl, 6ds. Change shuttles. *Shuttle 1*: Chain 5ds, pearl, 5ds, sm p, 3ds. RW. Continue pattern, joining to each pair of picots in Row 3. When finished, end off.

With a transparent sewing thread attach the lace to the covered metal ring before applying the stiffening medium. This will ensure the lace retains its size despite any shrinkage of the cotton. Shape the coronet, being careful to wipe any liquid off the pearls. Allow it to dry in a dust-free environment.

LIBERTY
A FREE WEB-LIKE DESIGN

Materials
1 or 2 shuttles
threads of selected colours and weights
variety of beads
crochet hook
sharp needle
tapestry needle
lace pins
metal ring, 25 cm (10 inches) in diameter
circle of calico, 35 cm (14 inches) in diameter

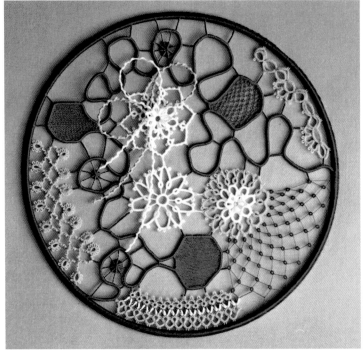

Liberty

Free design is quite interesting and absorbing. Somewhat like collage, it grows and changes as you go along. It challenges the experienced tatter to combine a variety of techniques with different threads and beads. 'Found objects' and spare motifs/braids can also be included. Some of these may create a three-dimensional effect. The stitches used in the design illustrated here include node (Victorian sets or ric-rac), spiral, mignonette (see pattern Victoriana on page 65), lattice work and padded tatting (see page 49), together with small pearls and silver rice beads. These are held together in a web-like design by needleworked bars.

You will need to sketch your design roughly in pencil on a piece of paper that will fit inside the circumference of your ring. Tat all the motifs, braids, cords and samples that you want to include as elements. Some of these will become features, while others will be secondary elements or fillers. Move them around till you have the arrangement you like best. Be prepared to change your original design.

Once you are happy with your arrangement, centre it on the calico and trace it lightly onto the fabric. Then tack the calico design to the back of the metal ring, ensuring it is stretched firmly in place. Firstly tack any main outer elements to the *ring only*, then tack the central arrangement to the calico. Lastly, tack down the fillers. (In this design the green padded cord was added last.) Now you are ready to make the needleworked bars with a tapestry needle without catching in the calico. Fill in any sections you wish. Let your imagination guide you, but keep a balance between the positive and negative spaces.

When all the bars are in place and the elements joined like a web, remove the calico backing. Do not yet remove the tacking which holds your lace to the metal ring. Finally, crochet around the ring to attach the web firmly, loosening the tacking as you proceed. Your design may be suspended against an appropriate background, or mounted in a support to be viewed alone.

GUM BLOSSOMS

Here is another free design which incorporates a piece of printed fabric. It consists of a variety of threads, including silver cord and softer cottons which are good for frayed picots. Most of the individual pieces are discrete rings. All the elements were stitched onto the backing fabric, but they could have been treated as a collage and glued on. A leaf-like insertion of lace has been added below the floral arrangement.

Gum blossoms

ANGEL FISH

Angel Fish, another free design, but a little more controlled, appears on page 10. It consists of rings, chains, mignonette (see pattern Victoriana, page 65), sequins and lots of beads. There is one larger, round, flat bead as an eye. This design was hand-stitched to a silk background before being framed.

PADDED TATTING TECHNIQUE

This technique is also known as pearl tatting. You will need 2 balls of thread the same thickness, one shuttle (preferably a large or Tatsy shuttle), a length of narrow cord, or several equal lengths of cotton which together will be treated as a cord.

Wind the cord onto the shuttle. If you are using several lengths of cotton, wind them on simultaneously as one cord.

Blue and black fleur-de-lis of padded tatting

Join the ends of the 2 balls of thread to the end of the cord. Then place the balls on opposite sides of the cord. Tat as if you were making a chain, but alternate between the balls of thread after each double stitch. This will produce ridges of lark's head knots on opposite sides of the cord. Needle tatters will have to tat directly onto the cord to avoid the bulk at the eye of the needle.

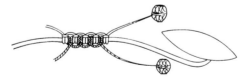

Padded tatting technique

Tat for as long as required. Picots can be added wherever you wish them. Two balls of different colours produce a striped effect. If you substitute shuttles of thread for the balls, you could add small Josephine rings (refer to Victoriana, row 7, on page 64) on the outside of the cord as you go along.

BRIANA
A THREE-DIMENSIONAL CHARMER

Materials
3 shuttles
No. 20 green
2 x No. 20 complementary colours
5 small beads

Briana

Here is a charming three-dimensional circular project for tatters who enjoy a challenge. It is composed of overlapping flowers and leaves. This piece is meant to be viewed from one side only so it has a definite right and wrong side. It can be mounted in a small frame or anywhere that takes your fancy.

The beads are for highlights only, so they need to be small. The choice of colours for the flowers is entirely up to you. For convenience, I have named the shuttles G (green), LC (light colour) and DC (dark colour). With shuttles LC and DC you tat the flowers traditionally, but with shuttle G you do reverse/wrong way tatting (WWT) along the stem and also make the 3 rings of traditional double stitches as leaves. The G thread forms a circular foundation behind the flowers, with the 3 leaves at intervals. Refer to Split Ring for wrong way tatting on page 20.

Wind the shuttles as follows:

G: 1.5 m/yds
LC: 2.75 m/yds and 2 beads
DC: 1.75 m/yds and 3 beads

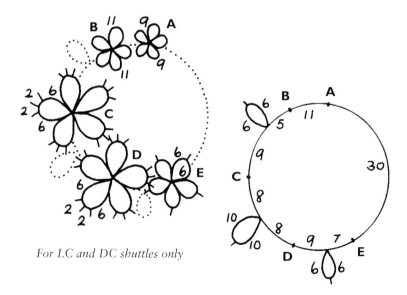

For LC and DC shuttles only

For G shuttle only

51

The first diagram gives the double stitch count for LC and DC shuttles, while the second diagram is for G shuttle only.

Begin at flower A with the LC. As you tat the 2nd petal, join in the G thread, and at the 3rd petal join in the DC thread. When the 5 petals are done place the G thread to the back of the flower and the DC thread to the front. Close the flower by looping the LC thread firmly between the first 2 petals, and then take it to the back of the work. Slide up 1 bead on the DC and position it over the centre of the flower. Then pass the DC across the flower to the back of the work as well.

Keeping LC and DC together, place them over your hand ready to tat a chain. Using WWT work 11ds with G shuttle. Make sure the first double stitch fits snugly behind flower A. Take up DC shuttle and tat flower B. Bring LC thread to the front and then close this flower firmly as before. Slide up a bead on LC and position this in the centre of flower B. Pass LC to the back of the work too. As before, keep LC and DC together and chain WWT with shuttle G for 5ds. Reverse work. With shuttle G only tat a ring of 6 normal ds, p, 6 normal ds to form a leaf. RW. Then take up LC and DC together again ready for a chain. With shuttle G chain a further 9ds in WWT.

Using LC tat flower C and, as before, bring DC to the front, close the flower and position a bead in the centre. With G shuttle tat a chain of 8ds in WWT over LC and DC. RW. Using G only make a ring of 10 normal ds, p, 10 normal ds. RW. Take up LC and DC again and in WWT with G tat a chain of 8ds. With LC make flower D as above, and position a bead from DC in the centre. With G make a chain of 9ds in WWT, a leaf of 6ds, p, 6ds normally, and a chain of 7ds in WWT. Work flower E with DC and a bead from LC. Then with G make a chain of 30ds WWT.

Now join the ends neatly behind flower A to form a circle. As in embroidery, very little of the LC and the DC should appear on the wrong side. These should be covered by the G thread. Turn to the front, arrange the flowers and block them before attaching to a suitable background.

SIOBHAN
AN ELEGANT TABLE CENTRE

Materials
2 shuttles or #7 needle
No. 40 thread
crochet hook

This tatted centre will look elegant on any polished surface or under glass. In No. 40 thread, it is 43 cm (17 inches) in diameter.

Siobhan table centre

It is composed of repeated rows and motifs. The motifs are tatted with two shuttles using the split ring technique, while the rest is tatted with one shuttle and a ball thread. While the centre illustrated is white, coloured threads could equally well be used, choosing threads of different values of the same colour and working from the darkest to the lightest in a sunburst effect.

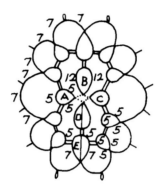

The motif

Motif: Rings A, B and C are tatted with Sh.1. Rings D and E are split rings, allowing work to proceed to the outer round without having to end off and start again. Refer to Split Ring technique on page 19. The motifs of Row 6 of the doily can be tatted separately earlier and attached when tatting Row 5. However, those of Row 3 must be tatted in order, as they have to be joined to one another.

Apart from the split ring technique for the motifs, the whole centre can be tatted with one shuttle or needle and a ball thread.

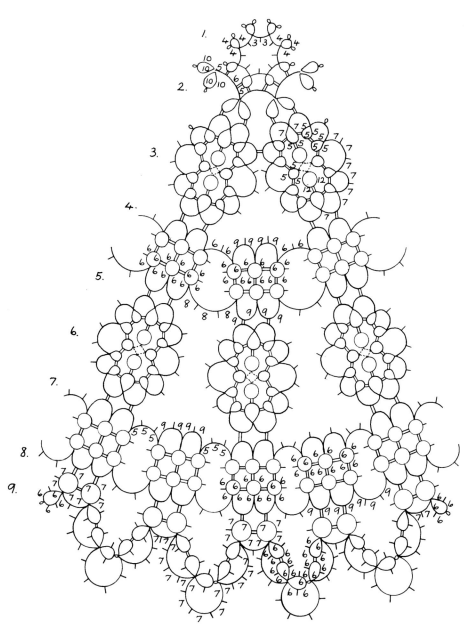

The doily

BORONIA
ALICE BAND WITH SEQUINS

Materials
1 shuttle or #5–#7 needle
padded Alice band
No. 20 thread of chosen colour
sequins to match
small beads to match
crochet hook
sewing thread

Boronia Alice band, side comb and button

Cute in pink, or any colour of your choice, this Alice band is sure to attract attention. The tatting is composed of motifs of two sizes on which sequins have been substituted for beads. Motif A is really a ring to which 6 sequins are added. Motif B adds a row of chain to Motif A and 12 sequins. As you thread the sequins make sure that they all face the same way. All rings have a small bead in the centre which is added to a formed picot. Refer to Methods 1, 2 and 4 on pages 16–18 of Techniques.

Sequins on motif A

Motif A: Only a shuttle wound with No. 20 thread is required. String the sequins in multiples of 6. Before starting each ring include 6 sequins in the thread you wrap around your hand. Tat the ring as if using beads and slide each sequin up into place when it is required. See Method 1. If you choose to place a small bead at the centre of each ring refer to Motif B and Method 4. A series of similar rings can be tatted without having to end off. Any length of thread between rings can be hidden behind the motifs as they are attached to the Alice band.

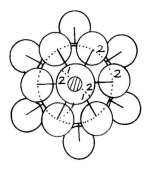

Sequins on Motif B

Motif B: For this motif you will need both shuttle and ball threads. String 12 sequins onto the ball thread and divide them into two sets of 6. Wind 50 cm (20 inches) CTM from the ball and slip one of the sets of 6 sequins onto the shuttle. Then using the shuttle alone, tat a central ring as for Motif A. Attach both the shuttle and the ball threads behind the last sequin of the ring. Tat a round of chains as illustrated (2ds, sequin, 2ds), sliding sequins from beside the ball when needed. See Method 2. This outer round of sequins will be off-set to those already inside. As you go, make shuttle/lock joins behind the sequins of the inner ring. End off with a reef knot to which a drop of glue can be added.

Tat as many motifs as will cover the Alice band in a crazy pattern. Use a transparent sewing thread to attach them to the fabric. These motifs can be used on other accessories also, such as side combs or the covered buttons of a jacket. Care needs to be taken when laundering these articles so that the sequins do not come into contact with a hot surface.

FESTIVA
SNOWFLAKE EARRINGS

Materials
1 shuttle or #5–#7 needle
No. 20 thread
36 seed beads
fine crochet hook
suitable earring findings
stiffening medium

White Festiva earrings with coloured beads

This is an easy pattern which may also be used to decorate windows, trees or gift cards for the festive season. It is tatted CTM. Tip to tip, it measures 3 cm (1¼ inches). For each snowflake you will require 12 beads for the chains and 6 loose ones for the rings. If you wish, the 12 beads for the chains may be a different colour from those between the rings. In this case, you will need 24 beads of one colour and 12 beads of the second colour.

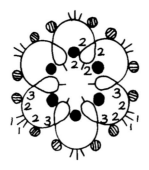

Festiva

Measure 1 m (1 yd) of thread from the ball. *Do not cut the thread*. String on the 12 beads for the chains and keep them close to the ball as you wind the length of thread onto the shuttle. Start at any ring and work 2ds, (p, 2ds) 3 times. RW. As you prepare to tat the first chain, slide 2 beads along the ball thread and keep them over the back of your fingers in readiness. Refer to Method 2 on page 17. Work the visual pattern, inserting beads as indicated. Vary the lengths of the picots to create the feathery appearance of a snowflake. RW.

The next 4 rings will be made as follows. Tat 2ds, pick up one of the loose beads on the end of the crochet hook and slide it onto the last picot of the preceding ring, make a picot join, 2ds, (p, 2ds) twice, cl ring. Refer to Method 3 on page 17. When tatting the 6th ring, you will have to slide a loose bead onto the last picot of ring 5 *and* the first picot of ring 1 before you make the picot joins. The remaining chains will be tatted the same way as the first.

Join the 6th chain to the base of ring 1 and end off.

Make a second snowflake to match, and stiffen both before mounting them on suitable jewellery findings.

VICTORIANA
A BEAUTIFUL BEADED BAG

Materials
2 shuttles or #5–#7 needle
No. 20/40 black or charcoal grey cotton, silk or rayon
fine crochet hook
black rice beads
small black beads
fabric for lining
ribbon for drawstrings

Victoriana

Here is a very different bag with a Victorian charm. Although illustrated in charcoal grey, it could just as easily be tatted in black, or in white for a bride. The daisy motifs in the middle form the foundation round of the bag. Everything else is worked in rounds upwards or downwards from there. Extra motifs can be added to enlarge the bag, and rounds of zigzagging rice beads may be added or deleted at will in order to lengthen or shorten it. Refer to Method 4 on page 18 for the placement of beads in the centres of the daisies and to Method 3 on page 17 for beads on the picots where the daisies join to one another and to the rows on either side of them. Method 5 on page 18 will help with the addition of beads on a separate thread, and Method 2 on page 17 helps with beads on the chain around the top.

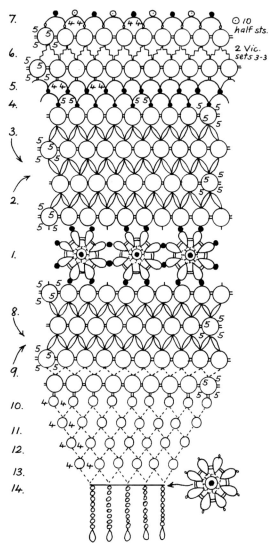

Visual pattern of bag

The bag illustrated was tatted in No. 20 cotton. It is 25 cm (10 inches) in circumference and 22 cm (9 inches) deep. There are 10 daisy motifs around the middle and one in the centre of the mignonette at the bottom.

Daisy pattern

Row 1: As many daisies as you require. Refer to Method 3 on page 17 for adding beads to picots as you join these together, and to Method 4 on page 18 for the placement of beads in the centres of the daisies.

Row 2: Use one shuttle. The beads that zigzag between the rings of this row are slipped into place once the rings are closed. Add the required number of rice beads to the shuttle thread before starting. Have a separate thread of rice beads ready to be attached by pairs to the upper rings as illustrated in Method 5 on page 18. All rings have 5ds, p/join, 5ds, p, 5ds, p, 5ds. As this row is joined to the picots of the daisies, small loose beads are slipped onto the picots with a crochet hook. See Method 3 on page 17.

Row 3: Use one shuttle. This row is the same as Row 2 in that beads on the shuttle thread are slipped into place after the rings are closed, but it is joined between the pairs of beads mentioned above from the other side of the separate thread. Refer to Method 5 on page 18.

Row 4: Continuous chains of 5ds, p, 5ds, with shuttle/lock joins to the picots of the adjacent rings in Row 3. Add beads to the picots before joining. See Method 3 on page 17.

Row 5: As for Row 4, but the chains are 4ds, p, 4ds.

Row 6: Use one shuttle and a ball thread. Between the rows of rings tat 2 Victorian sets (ricrac tatting) of 3—3. Each Victorian set consists of 3 first half-stitches followed by 3 second half-stitches.

Row 7: Small beads alternate with Josephine rings along the tops of the chains. Use two shuttles. Work out how many chains will be needed around the top, and then thread half as many beads onto shuttle 2. The Josephine rings, which contain 10 half-stitches, will be tatted with shuttle 2. You can use whichever half-stitch you find easier to make. Perhaps you would rather have only beads around the top. In this case use one shuttle and a ball thread. Place twice as many beads onto the ball thread, and tat 4ds, bead, 4ds for the chains, making shuttle/lock joins into the picots of the adjacent rings of Row 6.

Row 8: Work as for Row 2.

Row 9: Work as Row 3 without placing between the rings.

Row 10: First row of mignonette. The small rings of 4ds, join, 4ds, are joined to the picots of the adjacent rings in Row 9. There are measured spaces of 2 cm (¾ inch) each between the rings.

Rows 11–13: Mignonette, as above. At regular intervals begin decreasing by joining a ring to 2 measured spaces of thread. As you decrease the mignonette towards the bottom, you will have to bear in mind that a daisy of 8–10 petals will ultimately be joined to it.

Row 14: Daisy. There are two ways to attach the daisy to the mignonette: directly as you tat it, or indirectly by hand-sewing after the daisy itself is finished. The decorative strings of beads can be added to the tips of the daisy by hand later on.

Once the lace is complete, make a suitable fabric lining and attach this to the neck of the bag and to the daisy at the bottom. Thread 2 drawstrings through the lace. The ends of the drawstrings may be attached to small tassels or hidden inside decorative bobbles. The bobbles are actually padded balls made from small circles of fabric covered with seed beads. Run a thread around the edge of each circle, add a cotton ball to the centre and draw the fabric closed around it. Turn in any raw edges and end off. Attach the beads randomly.

MIGNONETTE

While we cannot be sure what exactly inspired the naming of this form of tatting, the word 'mignonette' is derived from the French *mignon, mignonne*, 'dainty, delicate, sweet'. There is a mignonette tree grown in Africa, Europe and Asia which has delicate grey-green leaves with a fine network. It is possible that this form of tatting took its name from this plant. The lace also resembles the more familiar, dainty maidenhair fern.

Although mignonette is seldom seen in contemporary tatting, it was relatively common in the latter half of the nineteenth century. Made with one shuttle only, mignonette simply consists of rows of tiny discrete rings joined to precisely measured spaces of considerable length in the previous row. The rings are free to move along the spaces. Mignonette may be tatted on the straight or in a circle. In order to appear delicate it is best done in a fine thread, such as 60 or 80 cotton.

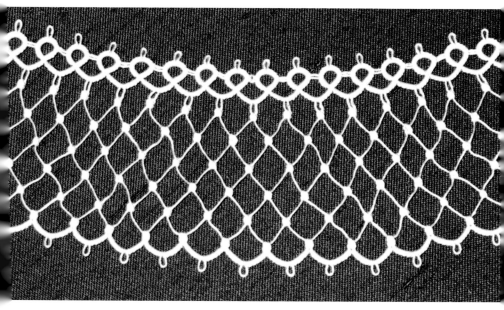

Mignonette

To increase in an expanding section of lace, the measured spaces may be made longer, or 2 rings can be joined to the same space. By applying the contemporary technique of split rings, a second shuttle may be brought into use to tat a split ring when progressing from one circular row to the next. This will keep everything regular and eliminate ending off.

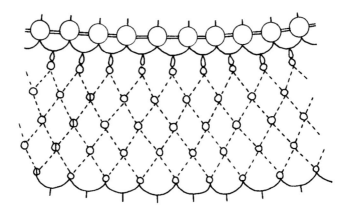

Mignonette

RINGLETS
THREE USES OF SPLIT RINGS

Split rings have become very popular with tatters all around the world. Not only do they save ending off and restarting in certain places, but they can also be used to form patterns that were once unattainable. The following three patterns all involve split rings to a lesser or greater degree. Refer to Split Ring technique on page 19.

INTERLACED MEDALLION

Interlaced medallion

In this medallion there is only one split ring. It could be left out altogether, but you would have to end off after the central ring and start again for Round 1. The technique where this split ring is involved is known as COOR—Climbing Out Of a Ring— and it will save time and energy. To put it into effect you will need two shuttles. With shuttle 1 tat the central ring with one fewer picots than required, in this case, 11. Then leave a space of thread the size of a picot before tatting one half of a ring in Round 1. With shuttle 2, leave a similar space and complete the other half ring in WWT. You now have the central ring, a false 12th picot, and the first ring of Round 1, all without ending off!

This medallion was worked in No. 20 threads of two different colours. It measures 6 cm (2½ inches) in diameter. Two shuttles were wound CTM from their respective balls. For this piece, shuttle 1 carries green thread and shuttle 2 carries white.

Quantities
Round 1: Shuttle 1: 1 m (40 inches); shuttle 2: 0.75 m (30 inches)
Round 2: 2 m (80 inches) on each shuttle

While the basic tatting is not difficult, proceed carefully in order to pass the coloured chains to the correct side of one another before joining the rings. To preserve definite right and wrong sides for viewing, the chains were tatted with the reverse order of half-stitches and all joins were made downward.

Interlaced medallion

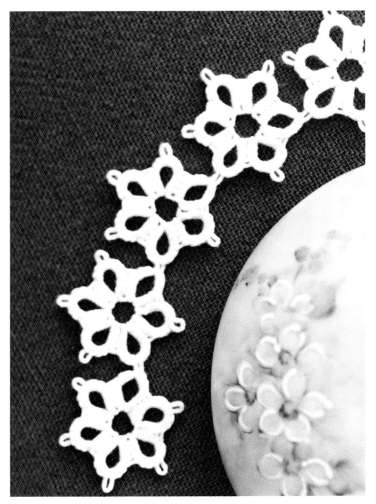

Daisy chain

Each of the daisies in this chain has 2 split rings—the ones that appear to be joined by a picot. In actual fact, the picot is false, being just a short space between the 2 'petals'. The other 4 petals are tatted normally with the shuttles on the respective sides. Use shuttle 1 to tat the major part of each daisy on the topside of the split rings, and shuttle 2 for the WWT of the split rings and the one ring between them on the downside. Reverse the order of the half-stitches for this one ring for shuttle 2 in order to maintain the same appearance of the double stitches for all the rings. The pattern illustrated was tatted in No. 20 cotton and is 2 cm ($^{7}/_{8}$ inch) wide, but any weight thread may be used for these daisies. Variegated thread or two analogous colours on the shuttles will produce a subtle shading across the petals.

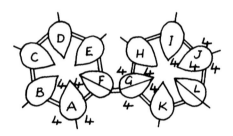

Daisy chain

NOUGHTS AND CROSSES

Noughts and crosses

Three shuttles are needed for this pattern, the third one being added to form the crisscrossing chains. The 'noughts' are a series of split rings end to end. These rings were tatted first and the 'crosses', the crisscrossing beaded chains, were joined on later. Each chain has 10 small beads. Refer to Method 2 on page 17.

All the rings and half the chains may be tatted with shuttles 1 and 2 without ending off, so place half the beads on shuttle 1 before starting the work. Tat the split rings of the first diagram, making a very small picot in the WWT section of each ring. As you make the last ring, tat three-quarters of it with shuttle 1 and the remaining quarter in WWT with shuttle 2. This brings both shuttles to the same position as the picots on the other rings.

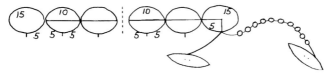

The noughts first ...

With the same side of the work upwards, consider shuttle 1 as a ball thread and place it around your hand. Then with shuttle 2 tat the first chain, sliding the beads into place as required. Skip one ring and attach the chain with a lock join to the picot of the next ring. Place the remaining half of the beads on a matching ball thread and then wind shuttle 3 CTM, keeping the beads beside the ball. With a lock join attach this new thread to the ring you skipped with shuttle 2. Tat a similar beaded chain to the first one. Before you join this chain to the next free picot, position shuttles 1 and 2 so that a crisscrossing of chains is effected. Refer to the second diagram. Continue making and joining chains, alternating them in the crisscross until the other end of the rings.

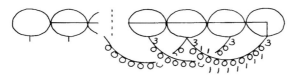

... then the crosses

The piece illustrated was worked in a variegated rayon equivalent to No. 10–15 cotton. It is 2 cm (⅞ inch) wide. It may be used on the straight or curved.

VALENTINA
A BEADED HEART

Materials
2 shuttles or #7 needle
No. 40 red crochet cotton
22 seed beads (optional)
fine crochet hook
triple-folded blank gift card
small piece of backing fabric
craft glue

Valentina

Here is a delightfully simple heart to enclose in a card for
Valentine's Day. It will surely be appreciated. Later it could be

included in a piece of patchwork as a keepsake. The heart itself measures 6 cm (2½ inches) in length and width, so your choice of card needs to allow for these dimensions.

Wind your shuttles CTM: on shuttle 1 wind on 3m (3¼ yds) and on shuttle 2 wind on 4 m (4½ yds). Have the 22 seed beads loose in a shallow container or on a piece of felt beside the fine crochet hook. Each bead will be added to a formed picot before two rings are joined together. Refer to Method 3 on page 17 for the addition of beads to formed picots using a crochet hook.

Start with shuttle 1, using shuttle 2 as a ball thread. As you tat ring A, grade the lengths of the picots so that the middle one is the longest. This helps to create a heart shape inside as

Heart diagram

well as outside. Follow the visual pattern, remembering to slip a seed bead onto each joining picot between rings. Make the join and continue with the ring. Note that rings B–G have 4ds, join, 2ds, p, 2ds, p, 4ds, whereas rings H–K have 3ds, join, 3ds, p, 3ds, p, 3ds. The tiny ring, M, will be tatted with shuttle 2. All chain spaces are 3ds, though the number of picots per chain varies. After ring M tat a matching side of the heart until you are at the top again. As you tat the last ring a second bead will have to be added as you make a picot join to ring A.

Once your heart is complete block it for a good shape. While it is drying you can prepare the card. Cut the piece of backing fabric to size and glue it in place. Then fold the card in order to glue one flap behind the fabric. Set the card aside to dry flat. When both the heart and the card are ready, arrange the lace in its place and lightly glue it. Add a suitable inscription.

FLEUR
A CHOKER WITH TATTED SQUARES

Materials
2 shuttles
No. 20 black thread
104 black rice/bugle beads
suitable clasp
medium safety pin
fine crochet hook
spacer, slightly wider than the length of the beads

*Fleur and
close-up detail*

74

Here is a lacy choker which involves split rings and tatted squares. Refer to pages 19 and 22 for detailed instructions on both of these. The length of this choker is 33 cm (13 inches), not including the clasp. If you wish to shorten it, remove 6 beads for each ring + square unit you delete from the pattern. The width is approximately 2.5 cm (1 inch). All beads are loose, to be placed on formed picots later. Refer to Method 3 on page 17. There should be a definite right and a wrong side to this piece, so keep the right side uppermost for the entire piece.

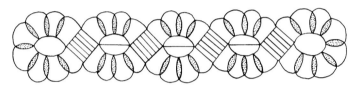

Choker braid

There are two rows to this pattern:
Row 1: the squares and the split rings with 6 measured picots (7 on the ends)
Row 2: a continuous chain and placement of the beads.

For Row 1 wind both your shuttles CTM: shuttle 1 with 6 m (6½ yds), and shuttle 2 with 5 m (5½ yds). Measure the length of your rice or bugle beads and then cut a spacer of sufficient width that your closed picots will be just slightly longer than the beads.

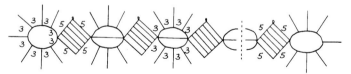

Row 1

With shuttle 1 tat a normal ring with 7 measured picots. Insert the safety pin between the threads of the two shuttles to reserve a small space. Work one tatted square of 5 rows of 5ds. Follow this with a split ring of 3ds, mp, 3ds, mp, 3ds, mp, 3ds on each

75

side of the ring, then another tatted square.

One ring–one square forms the basic unit of this pattern, approximately 2 cm (³/₄ inch) long. It may be repeated for the length required for your choker, but always complete the tatted square. Then finally, with shuttle 1, tat a normal ring the same as the first ring with 7 measured picots. End off.

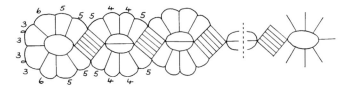

Row 2

For Row 2 you will require only one shuttle and the ball thread CTM. Wind 2 m (80 inches) on the shuttle. *Do not cut the thread.* Have all the rice or bugle beads and the fine crochet hook ready. With the right side of the work facing up, start with a shuttle join at the corner of a tatted square on the side of Row 1. Keep your tension firm for this row so that the chains will curve nicely. Chain 5ds. Then place one bead onto the end of the crochet hook, slip it onto the first measured picot and make a shuttle/lock join. Chain 4ds and place a bead on the next picot in a similar fashion. Chain 4ds and place a third bead as before. Chain a further 5ds and then make a shuttle join into the tip of the next square.

Continue this pattern along the side of your choker to the last square. Then work around the end ring with 7mp, tatting the respective chains. Depending on the type of jewellery clasp you want, a couple of picots could be added to the chains at the end so the clasp may be attached later. See the above diagram for the chains of 3ds, p, 3ds. Work along the other side, placing beads on the remaining picots. When you complete Row 2 end off neatly. Attach your chosen jewellery findings and/or clasp.

USEFUL REFERENCES

Connors, Judith: *Beads in Tatting*, Kangaroo Press, Sydney 1997

Foster, Barbara: *Learn Needle Tatting Step-by-step*, Handy Hands Inc., Paxton IL 1998

Haan-Van Beek, To De: *New Dimensions in Tatting*, Kangaroo Press, Sydney 1994

Ikuta, Mituko: *Tatting and Bead Tatting 1*, Japan Publications, Japan 1994

Ikuta, Mituko: *Tatting and Bead Tatting 2*, Japan Publications, Japan 1995

Jones, Rebecca: *The Complete Book of Tatting*, Kangaroo Press, Sydney 1985

Konior, Mary: *Tatting with Visual Patterns*, Kangaroo Press, Sydney 1992

Libin, Nina: *Tatted Lace of Beads, The Techniques of Beanile Lace*, Lacis Publications, Berkeley CA 1998

Morin, Selma & Ed: *The Complete Book of Jiffy Needle Tatting*, KC Publishing Inc., Kansas City 1992

Nicholls, Elgiva: *Tatting: Technique and History*, reprint by Dover Publications, NY 1984

Peel, Rosemarie: *Tatting with Beads*, Lacet Publications, Nuneaton, England 1997

INDEX

BIOGRAPHY

JUDITH CONNORS is an experienced tatter who delights in sharing her interest and enthusiasm for tatting with others. An accredited teacher with the Australian Lace Guild, she contributes to many Australian and international publications. She collects old lace and has a particular interest in the history of tatting and tatters. In her spare time, she traces her family tree. Judith lives in Brisbane, Australia.

LACIS publishes and distributes books specifically related to the textile arts, focusing on the subjects of lace and lace making, costume, embroidery and hand sewing.

Other LACIS books of interest:
THE CARE AND PRESERVATION OF TEXTILES, Karen Finch & Greta Putnam
THE ART OF HAIR WORK, Mark Campbell
SMOCKING & FINE SEWING, ed by Jules & Kaethe Kliot
MILLINERY FOR EVERY WOMAN, Georgina Kerr Kaye
TECHNIQUE OF LADIESí HAIR DRESSING (19th c.): Campbell & Mallemont
KNITTING: 19th c. Sources: ed. Jules & Kaethe Kliot
HAUTE COUTURE EMBROIDERY: THE ART OF LESAGE, Palmer White
THE MARY FRANCES SEWING BOOK, Jane Eayre Fryer
THE MARY FRANCES KNITTING & CROCHETING BOOK, Jane Eayre Fryer
THE MARY FRANCES HOUSEKEEPER, Jane Eayre Fryer
THE MARY FRANCES COOK BOOK, Jane Eayre Fryer
THE MARY FRANCES GARDEN BOOK, Jane Eayre Fryer
BATTENBERG LACE PATTERN BOOK, ed. Jules & Kaethe Kliot
NETTING: From Early Sources, ed. Jules & Kaethe Kliot
CROCHET: EDGINGS & INSERTIONS, Eliza A. Taylor & Belle Robinson
CROCHET: EDGINGS & MORE, ed. Jules & Kaethe Kliot
CROCHET: NOVELTIES, ed. Jules & Kaethe Kliot
CROCHET: MORE EDGINGS, ed. Jules & Kaethe Kliot
CROCHET: DOLLS & NOVELTIES, ed. Jules & Kaethe Kliot
THE NEEDLE MADE LACES OF RETICELLA. ed Jules & Kaethe Kliot
CASALGUIDI STYLE LINEN EMBROIDERY, Effie Mitrofanis
CUTWORK, HEDEBO & BRODERIE ANGLAISE, ed Jules & Kaethe Kliot
THE ART OF SHETLAND LACE, Sarah Don
CREATING ORIGINAL HAND-KNITTED LACE, Margaret Stove
BERLIN WORK, SAMPLERS & EMBROIDERY OF 19TH C. Raffaella Serena
THE MAGIC OF FREE MACHINE EMBROIDERY, Doreen Curran
DESIGNS FOR CHURCH EMBROIDERIES, Thomas Brown & Son
CROSS-STITCH ALPHABETS & TREASURES, ed. by Jules & Kaethe Kliot
EMBROIDERY WITH BEADS, Angela Thompson
BEADED BAGS AND MORE, ed. by Jules & Kaethe Kliot
BEAD EMBROIDERY, Joan Edwards
BEAD EMBROIDERY, Valerie Campbell-Harding and Pamela Watts
INNOVATIVE BEADED JEWELRY TECHNIQUES, Gineke Root
BEADED ANIMALS IN JEWELRY, Letty Lammens and Els Scholte
CLASSIC BEADED PURSE PATTERNS, E. de Jong-Kramer
BEAD WEAVING: ACCESSORIES, Takako Sako
BEAD WEAVING, ELEGANCE, Takako Sako
LOCKER HOOKING, Leone Peguero
DMC BOOK OF CHARTED TATTING DESIGNS, Kirstine & Inge Nikolajsen
TATTED LACE OF BEADS: TECHNIQUE OF BEANILE LACE, Nina Libin
TATTING: DESIGNS FROM VICTORIAN LACE, ed.by Jules & Kaethe Kliot
THE ART OF TATTING, Katherine Hoare
TATTING WITH VISUAL PATTERNS, Mary Konior
PRACTICAL TATTING, Phyllis Sparks
NEW DIMENSIONS IN TATTING, To de Haan-van Beek
THE ART OF NETTING, Jules & Kaethe Kliot
BEADS IN TATTING, Judith Connors
TENERIFFE LACE, Jules & Kaethe Kliot

For a complete list of LACIS titles, write to:

LACIS
3163 Adeline Street, Berkeley, CA 94703   USA